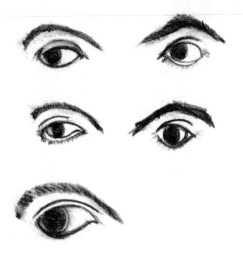

Momo's Press San Francisco 1979

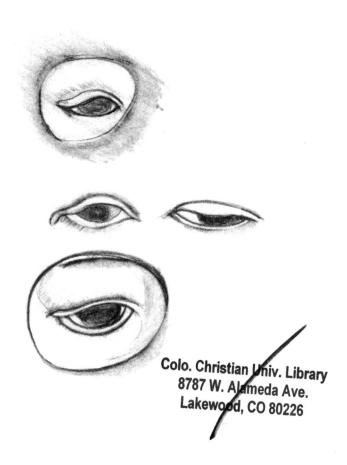

Lorca / Blackburn · Poems
of Federico García Lorca
chosen and translated by
Paul Blackburn

The cover and inside drawings are by Basil King. Design and composition at Spring Creek. Library of Congress Catalog Card Number: 78-78274. Copyright © 1979 by Joan Blackburn and the Estate of Federico García Lorca. ISBN 0-917672-08-9 (paper) 0-917672-09-7 (cloth). Momo's Press gratefully acknowledges the support and participation of Harry Lewis, George Economou, Basil King, Joan Blackburn and Holbrook Teter in the production of this volume. This book was partially funded by the National Endowment for the Arts. Momo's Press, P.O. Box 14061, San Francisco, California 94114.

Library of Congress Cataloging in Publication Data
García Lorca, Federico, 1898-1936.
    Lorca/Blackburn : poems of Federico García Lorca.
    I. Blackburn, Paul.
PQ6613.A763A22   1979   861'.6'2   78-78274
ISBN 0-917672-09-7
ISBN 0-917672-08-9 pbk.

Forward

So far as I have been able to ascertain, these versions of Lorca represent the latest ones Blackburn made before his death on September 13, 1971. He was continuously "working" them. My comparative reading of them against other versions (published & unpublished) and the original texts (*Obras Completas*, Madrid: Aguilar, 1954) confirms the efficacy of his special intelligence and instincts as a poet-translator. The changes invariably reveal moves in the interests of economy, melody, and accuracy; therefore, I have invariably accepted the later readings — except for restoring what appears to have been an inadvertently omitted stanza in the *Ode to Salvador Dali* (for the record, the second to last one). To my knowledge, the only point at which a Blackburn rendition does not "square" with the original comes in the first stanza of *Canción de Jinete* (1860) in which he translates *bandoleros* as "stirrups." I note it here, not so much because it is inexplicable — an equivalence through synecdoche — as it is atypical, and let it stand.

The order of the poems does not always follow that of the Aguilar edition, there being considerations other than strict chronology in the planning of a book such as this.

Thanks are offered to Stavros Deligiorgis, Harry Lewis, and Jeanne Sanchez, who helped in different ways.

George Economou
January, 1979
New York City

Introduction

No modern Spanish poet has so seduced the English-speaking world as Federico García Lorca. Some of the reasons are best forgotten — the political capital made out of his death, for example, or the fact that at times he coincides with some of our tackier fantasies about "Spain." The real basis of his impact, however, is surely his concentrated lyric energy. At once daring and traditional, stark and explosive, his poetry seems to hold vast worlds of violence and sexuality in momentary, volatile equilibrium:

> Paint me with your blood-reddened
> mouth a heaven of love, in
> a depth of flesh the dark
> star of pain.

The poem in which these lines appear, "Madrigal de verano," is characteristic of Lorca's work in many ways. It begins with echoes of popular song and brilliant primary colors, then projects a stylized Andalusian landscape:

> That red mouth of yours, Estrella, gypsy,
> bring it close to mine, I
> will bite the apple
> > under this sungold noonday light!
> There's a moorish tower
> in the green olive grove on the hill, the color
> of your country flesh.   it tastes
> of honey and dawn.

The gypsy Estrella, with her double charge of pleasure and pain (her name is echoed as "star of pain" or "*estrella de dolor*" in the original), is also Lorca's necessary muse:

> My andalusian pegasus is
> captive of your open eyes;
> should he see them dead, his flight
> would be sullen, desolate.

In addition, she is linked to the murderous Danaides of Greek mythology. The poem thus sweeps us through a variety of tones held together by a climate of mingled lust and fear and by a dazzling, primal imagery (mouth, apple, dawn, lily, wheat, breasts) that suggests folk poetry in general and the Mediterranean folk tradition in particular.

Lorca was both a student and a practitioner of this tradition. Unlike his North American contemporaries, he never tried to make *poetry* out of modern industrial life. When he mentions the world most Europeans inhabit, as he does at the beginning of "Ode to Salvador Dali," his purpose is to condemn it:

> Man
> stomps the flagstoned streets. Mirrors
> avoid the reflection's magic.
> The government's closed down the perfume shops.
> A machine perpetuates its double beats.

This bleak, paved-over world is then contrasted with another mythological landscape, Catalan this time instead of Andalusian and hence a bit softer than in "Madrigal de verano":

> Cadaqués, set on the compass points between
> the water and the hill, mounts flights of stairs and
>   hides
> snails. Wooden flutes calm the air. An ancient
> woods-god gives fruits to the children.

Surely this is part of Lorca's fascination for us. Ever since Walt Whitman, our poets have been obliged to seek images of pure beauty within the industrial world we inhabit. Blackburn himself often sought and found fleeting moments of loveliness within modern city life. The truth is that we have very little choice. Since we live with our backs to the past, our only alternative would be silence. Lorca, on the other hand, often seems most relaxed and alive when he is writing ballads like "Canción de Jinete," whose only non-traditional feature is its slightly elliptical imagery:

In the black
moon of stirrups
the spurs sing.
        Little black horse,
Where do you carry your dead rider?

Or again, in a poem like "August," he stays close to the nursery-rhymes that influenced him in his youth:

August.
Counterpoints
sugar & peach, and
the sun in the afternoon
like the pit in a fruit.
The corn keeps intact
its smile, yellow, hard.
August.
The kids eat
dark bread, rich moon.

Why is a modest poem like this one so successful? For one thing, because of its bright, hard imagery. It's almost all nouns — tangible, everyday words that pile up, evoking the long, hot days of childhood summers. The first adjectives don't appear till the second stanza, when the natural world reveals its "smile." The possibility that this smile might be too sweet is sidestepped by the grinning row of corn-kernels, a whimsical but vivid picture with a kind of comic-book grotesqueness, and by the words "yellow" and "hard." The poem ends with a swift plunge into mystery on which its sense of implied depths depends. Without breaking the tone he has established in the first two stanzas, Lorca's image of "dark bread, rich moon" also opens out other, more suggestive worlds in which dream and reality briefly touch and color each other. Poems like "August" must also have been part of Lorca's attraction for Blackburn who, like many North American poets, often reached for a maximum of suggestiveness with a hard compression of phrasing.

Like Lorca himself, the culture about and for which he spoke was an accidental victim of the Spanish Civil War. The arrival of the consumer age and tourism, along with the mass exodus of Andalusians themselves, have made it unlikely that another figure of his type will appear. For all his considerable learning and formal sophistication, he remained essentially a folk poet whose roots seemed to reach back to a distant Minoan past.

Blackburn's translations catch this essential quality. Despite some quibbles, I find them splendid, full of the keen sense of words' sound and touch that characterized his own poetry. One example, among many, would be the line in "Ode to Salvador Dali":

> El hombre pisa fuerte las calles enlosadas
> Man stomps the flagstoned streets.

A *losa* is indeed a flagstone (or gravestone), but *enlosadas* could also be translated as "paved." Blackburn chooses the longer but more vivid "flagstoned," while shortening *"pisa fuerte"* (literally "treads heavily") to the stronger "stomps." Small decisions like these, so close to the ones involved in writing original verse, make up the real art of translation. Blackburn, as his versions of Occitan poetry have already shown, was one of the art's recent masters. In mingling his voice with Lorca's, he has done us all a service.

David H. Rosenthal

Lorca / Blackburn

Madrigal

1919

Yo te miré a los ojos
cuando era niño y bueno.
Tus manos me rozaron
y me diste un beso.

(Los relojes llevan la misma cadencia,
y las noches tienen las mismas estrellas.)

Y se abrió mi corazón
como una flor bajo el cielo,
los pétalos de lujuria
y los estambres de sueño.

(Los relojes llevan la misma cadencia,
y las noches tienen las mismas estrellas.)

En mi cuarto sollozaba
como el príncipe del cuento
por Estrellita de oro
que se fué de los torneos.

(Los relojes llevan la misma cadencia,
y las noches tienen las mismas estrellas.)

Yo me alejé de tu lado
queriéndote sin saberlo.
No sé cómo son tus ojos,
tus manos ni tus cabellos.
Sólo me queda en la frente
la mariposa del beso.

(Los relojes llevan la misma cadencia,
y las noches tienen las mismas estrellas.)

Madrigal

1919

> I looked at you, in your eyes,
> when I was a boy and kind.
> Your hands brushed against me
> and you gave me a kiss.

(Clocks keep the same cadence
and nights have the same stars.)

> My heart opened itself like
> a flower under the sky;
> petals of lubricity,
> stamen of drowsiness.

(Clocks keep the same cadence
and nights have the same stars.)

> I was sobbing in my room
> like the prince in the story
> for the proud lady
> who left the tournament.

(Clocks keep the same cadence
and nights have the same stars.)

> I left your side
> wanting you without knowing it
> I do not know what your hands are
> like, your eyes, your hair.
> On my forehead all that's left,
> the butterfly of a kiss.

(Clocks keep the same cadence
and nights have the same stars.)

Oda a Salvador Dalí

Una rosa en el alto jardín que tú deseas.
Una rueda en la pura sintaxis del acero.
Desnuda la montaña de niebla impresionista.
Los grises oteando sus balaustradas últimas.

Los pintores modernos, en sus blancos estudios,
cortan la flor aséptica de la raíz cuadrada.
En las aguas del Sena un *iceberg* de mármol
enfría las ventanas y disipa las yedras.

El hombre pisa fuerte las calles enlosadas.
Los cristales esquivan la magia del reflejo.
El Gobierno ha cerrado las tiendas de perfume.
La máquina eterniza sus compases binarios.

Una ausencia de bosques, biombos y entrecejos
yerra por los tejados de las casas antiguas.
El aire pulimenta su prisma sobre el mar
y el horizonte sube como un gran acueducto.

Marineros que ignoran el vino y la penumbra
decapitan sirenas en los mares de plomo.
La Noche, negra estatua de la prudencia, tiene
el espejo redondo de la luna en su mano.

Un deseo de formas y límites nos gana.
Viene el hombre que mira con el metro amarillo.
Venus es una blanca naturaleza muerta
y los coleccionistas de mariposas huyen.

❋

Cadaqués, en el fiel del agua y la colina,
eleva escalinatas y oculta caracolas.
Las flautas de madera pacifican el aire.
Un viejo dios silvestre da frutas a los niños.

Ode to Salvador Dali

One rose in the high garden you desire.
A single wheel in the pure syntax of steel.
The mountain stripped of impressionist fog.
Greys overlooking their final balustrades.

Modern painters in their white studios
cut the aseptic flower of the root squared.
In the Seine's waters a marble iceberg chills
windows, the ivy shrivels.   Man

stomps the flagstoned streets. Mirrors
avoid the reflection's magic.
The government's closed down the perfume shops.
A machine perpetuates its double beats.

No woods, screens, frowns; mint
growing on the roofs of old houses. Air
polishes its prism upon the sea & the horizon
rises like a great aqueduct.

Sailors, unknowing of the vine and the line between
light and shadow, decapitate sirens on leaden seas.
Night, that black statue of prudence, holds
the rounded mirror of moon between her palms.

A desire for forms and limits wins us over.
The man with the yellow meter-measure comes.
Venus is a white still-life
    & butterfly collectors
       run.

     ❀

Cadaques, set on the compass-point between
the water and the hill, mounts flights of stairs and hides
snails. Wooden flutes calm the air. An ancient
woods-god gives fruits to the children.

Sus pescadores duermen, sin ensueño, en la arena.
En alta mar les sirve de brújula una rosa.
El horizonte virgen de pañuelos heridos
junta los grandes vidrios del pez y de la luna.

Una dura corona de blancos bergantines
ciñe frentes amargas y cabellos de arena.
Las sirenas convencen, pero no sugestionan,
y salen si mostramos un vaso de agua dulce.

❋

¡Oh Salvador Dalí, de voz aceitunada!
No elogio tu imperfecto pincel adolescente
ni tu color que ronda la color de tu tiempo,
pero alabo tus ansias de eterno limitado.

Alma higiénica, vives sobre mármoles nuevos.
Huyes la oscura selva de formas increíbles.
Tu fantasía llega donde llegan tus manos,
y gozas el soneto del mar en tu ventana.

El mundo tiene sordas penumbras y desorden,
en los primeros términos que el humano frecuenta.
Pero ya las estrellas ocultando paisajes,
señalan el esquema perfecto de sus órbitas.

La corriente del tiempo se remansa y ordena
en las formas numéricas de un siglo y otro siglo.
Y la Muerte vencida se refugia temblando
en el círculo estrecho del minuto presente.

Al coger su paleta, con un tiro en un ala,
pides la luz que anima la copa del olivo.
Ancha luz de Minerva, constructora de andamios,
donde no cabe el sueño ni su flora inexacta.

Its fishermen sleep dreamless on the sand.
A rose serves them as compass on the seas.
The clean horizon of wounded handkerchiefs
conjoins the great windows of fish and moon.

A harsh crown of white brigs invests
bitter foreheads and shocks of sandy hair.
The sirens convince but make no suggestion,
and if we show them a glass of fresh water, they go.

❀

O Salvador Dali, your voice olive-dark!
I do not praise the adolescent imperfection of your brush
or your color which guards the color of your time,
but I commend your everlastingly circumscribed longings.

Hygienic mind, you live above new marble pillars.
You flee the dark wood of incredible forms.
Your imagination attains wherever your hands arrive,
you take pleasure from the sonnet of the sea at your window.

The world contains
voiceless partial shadows
and riot
in those foregrounds man frequents.
But concealing landscapes, the stars
        now make known
the perfect diagram of their orbits.

The current of time eddies, arranges itself
in the numerical rituals of one century and another.
And Death, subdued, trembling takes shelter in
the narrow circle of the passing minute.

In picking up your palette with the aim of a wing,
you invoke the light which informs the
        crown of the living olive.
Wide-flung light of Minerva, builder of scaffolds,
upon which is no room for the dream
        nor for your inaccurate flora.

Pides la luz antigua que se queda en la frente,
sin bajar a la boca ni al corazón del hombre.
Luz que temen las vides entrañables de Baco
y la fuerza sin orden que lleva el agua curva.

Haces bien en poner banderines de aviso,
en el límite oscuro que relumbra de noche.
Como pintor no quieres que te ablande la forma
el algodón cambiante de una nube imprevista.

El pez en el pecera y el pájaro en la jaula.
No quieres inventarlos en el mar o en el viento.
Estilizas o copias después de haber mirado
con honestas pupilas sus cuerpecillos ágiles.

Amas una materia definida y exacta
donde el hongo no pueda poner su campamento.
Amas la arquitectura que construye en lo ausente
y admites la bandera como una simple broma.

Dice el compás de acero su corto verso elástico
Desconocidas islas desmiente ya la esfera.
Dice la línea recta su vertical esfuerzo
y los sabios cristales cantan sus geometrías.

＊

Pero también la rosa del jardín donde vives.
¡Siempre la rosa, siempre, norte y sur de nosotros!
Tranquila y concentrada como una estatua ciega,
ignorante de esfuerzos soterrados que causa.

Rosa pura que limpia de artificios y croquis
y nos abre las alas tenues de la sonrisa.
(Mariposa clavada que medita su vuelo.)
Rosa del equilibrio sin dolores buscados.
¡Siempre la rosa!

You invoke the ancient light which rests on the forehead
not reaching down to the man's mouth or his heart.
Light which the innermost vines of Bacchus fear
and the masterless force that curving water has.

You do well, friend, to put in warning flags
on the dark border which glistens in the night.
As painter, you do not want the form to soften you,
the changing iridescent cotton of an unforseen cloud.

The fish in the fishbowl and the bird in the cage.
You do not wish to devise them in the sea or in the wind.
You stylize or you copy after having, with honest eyes,
looked at their small agile bodies.

You love a matter defined and exact, mushroom
may not pitch its tent there, you love
architecture which builds upon the absent and
you accept the banner with a simple joke.

The thud of steel recites its short resilient line.
Undiscovered islands now contradict the sphere.
        The straight line
speaks its vertical power
        and learned mirrors
sing their geometries.

                ❋

But in the garden where you live, also the rose.
Always the rose, always, north and south of us!
Concentrated, quiet as a blind statue, not knowing the
subterranean forces which occasion it.

        Pure rose,
it cleanses in rough drafts and craftsmanship
and opens to us the delicate wings of the smile.
(The butterfly mounted, contemplating its flight.)
Rose of equilibrium, not looking for pangs.
        The rose, always!

✳

¡Oh Salvador Dalí, de voz aceitunada!
Digo lo que me dicen tu persona y tus cuadros.
No alabo tu imperfecto pincel adolescente,
pero canto la firme dirección de tus flechas.

Canto tu bello esfuerzo de luces catalanas,
tu amor a lo que tiene explicación posible.
Canto tu corazón astronómico y tierno,
de baraja francesa y sin ninguna herida.

Canto el anisa de estatua que persigues sin tregua,
el miedo a la emoción que te aguarda en la calle.
Canto la sirenita de la mar que te canta
contada en bicicleta de corales y conchas.

Pero ante todo canto un común pensamiento
que nos une en las horas oscuras y doradas.
No es el Arte la luz que nos ciega los ojos.
Es primero el amor, la amistad o la esgrima.

Es primero que el cuadro que paciente dibujas
el seno de Teresa, la de cutis insomne,
el apretado bucle de Matilde la ingrata,
nuestra amistad pintada como un juego de oca.

Huellas dactilográficas de sangre sobre el oro
rayen el corazón de Cataluña eterna.
Estrellas como puños sin halcón te relumbren,
mientras que tu pintura y tu vida florecen.

No mires la clepsidra con alas membranosas,
ni la dura guadaña de las alegorías.
Viste y desnuda siempre tu pincel en el aire,
frente a la mar poblada con barcos y marinos.

❃

O Salvador Dali, your voice olive-dark!
I speak only what you and your canvases tell me. I
do not praise the adolescent imperfection of your brush,
but I sing the firm direction of your arrows.

I sing your beautiful spirit full of Catalan lights,
your love of what has possible explanation.
I sing your heart, astronomical and tender,
out of the French deck and with no tear whatsoever.

I sing the statue's longing you pursue without let,
fear for the emotion which awaits you in the street.
I sing the small siren of the sea who sings to you
          from a bicycle of conch and coral.

But I sing above all a common thought which
unites us in dark or golden hours. Art
is not the light that blinds our eyes. It is
love first, or friendship, or fencing.

It is first that the painting you sketch so patiently,
Teresa's breast, she with the restless flesh,
the tight curl of ungrateful Matilda, it's our
friendship painted as a game of dice.

Typewriter tracks of blood set upon gold
underline the heart of Catalunya eternal.
Stars like fists without falcons make you glitter
while your painting and your life flower.
You may not see the hourglass

          its membranous wings,
nor the hard scythe, tough with its allegories.
You saw it, and naked always, your brush in the air,
face to the sea,
          peopled with boats,
                    the men who sail them.

Los Cuatro Muleros

1

De los cuatro muleros,
que van al campo,
el de la mula torda,
moreno y alto.

2

De los cuatro muleros,
que van al agua,
el de la mula torda,
me roba el alma.

3

De los cuatro muleros,
que van al rio;
el de la mula torda,
es mi marío.

4

A qué buscas la lumbre
la calle arriba
si de tu cara sale
la brasa viva.

The Four Muleteers

Of those four men with mules
heading out to the fields,
the one with the dappled mule,
dark and tall.

Of those four men with mules
going down to water,
the one with the dappled mule
robbed my soul.

Of those four men with mules
heading down to the river,
the one with the dappled mule
is my husband.

Why do you borrow fire
in the street above,
when in your soot-streaked face
those coals live?

Madrigal de Verano

Agosto de 1920
(Vega de Zujaira)

Junta tu roja boca con la mía,
¡oh Estrella la gitana!
Bajo el oro solar del mediodía
morderé la manzana.

En el verde olivar de la colina,
hay una torre mora,
del color de tu carne campesina
que sabe a miel y aurora.

Me ofreces en tu cuerpo requemado,
el divino alimento
que da flores al cauce sosegado
y luceros al viento.

¿Cómo a mí te entregaste, luz morena?
¿Por qué me diste llenos
de amor tu sexo de azucena
y el rumor de tus senos?

¿No fué por mi figura entristecida?
(¡Oh mis torpes andares!)
¿Te dió lástima acaso de mi vida,
marchita de cantares?

¿Cómo no has preferido a mis lamentos
los muslos sudorosos
de un San Cristóbal campesino, lentos
en el amor y hermosos?

Madrigal de Verano

August, 1920
(Zujaira meadow)

That red mouth of yours, Estrella, gypsy,
bring it close to mine, I
will bite the apple
      under this sungold noonday light!

There's a moorish tower
in the green olive grove on the hill, the color
of your country flesh   it tastes
of honey & dawn.

Your flesh does, & you offer me
your doubly sunburnt body, the
holy food
makes flowers in the brookbed, quiet, blaze of
morning stars to the wind.

Tawny light,
why give yourself to me, why
give me your cunt full of lilies
& love &
      the sound of your breasts moving?

Not because of my sorry figure, my
slow, lumpy walk?
My life maybe,
seared by songs
hurt you?

Instead of my moaning, why
not prefer the
thighs of a San Cristobal peasant,
      sweating & slow in love, & handsome?

Danaide del placer eres conmigo.
Femenino Silvano.
Huelen tus besos como huele el trigo
reseco del verano.

Entúrbiame los ojos con tu canto.
Deja tu cabellera
extendida y solemne como un manto
de sombra en la pradera.

Píntame con tu boca ensangrentada
un cielo del amor,
en un fondo de carne la morada
estrella de dolor.

Mi pegaso andaluz está cautivo
de tus ojos abiertos;
volará desolado y pensativo
cuando los vea muertos.

Y aunque no me quisieras te querría
por tu mirar sombrío,
como quiere la alondra al nuevo día,
sólo por el rocío.

Junta tu roja boca con la mía,
¡oh Estrella la gitana!
Déjame bajo el claro mediodía
consumir la manzana.

The first night
the Danaides killed their husbands, it's
like that, you goddess of woods, your
kisses smell like wheat when it's
        dried by the summer.

Muddy my eyes with your song. Let
your hair fall, hang long & formal
as a cape spread, a shadow
upon the pasture.

Paint me with your blood-reddened
mouth a heaven of love, in
a depth of flesh the dark
star of pain.

My andalusian pegasus is
captive of your open eyes;
should he see them dead, his flight
would be sullen, desolate.

And should you not love me, I
would love you for your shadowed glance,
as lark loves the new day
for the dew alone.

Bring your red mouth close
to mine, Estrella, gypsy!
In the clear light of mid day
I will eat the apple. Let me!

Canción con Movimiento

Ayer.

(Estrellas
azules.)

Mañana.

(Estrellitas
blancas.)

Hoy.

Sueño flor adormecida
en el valle de la enagua.)

Ayer.

(Estrellas
de fuego.)

Mañana.

(Estrellas
moradas.)

Hoy.

Este corazón, ¡Dios mío!
¡Este corazón que salta!

Ayer.

(Memoria
de estrellas.

Mañana.

(Estrellas cerradas.)

Hoy . . .

(¡Mañana!)

¿Me marearé quizá
sobre la barca?
¡Oh los puentes del Hoy
en el camino de agua!

Song with a Particular Movement

Yesterday.

    (Stars
blue.)

        Tomorrow.

    (Little stars
white.)

        Today.

    (I dream of the flower sleeping
in the valley under the petticoat.)

        Yesterday.

    (Stars
of fire.)

        Tomorrow.

    (Purple
stars.)

        Today.

    This heart, O my Christ!
This heart of mine keeps jumping!

        Yesterday.

    (Remembering
stars.)

        Tomorrow.

    (Stars
thick, closed.)

        Today . . .

        (Tomorrow!)

I'll probaby get sick on the boat.
Today's bridges / on the road of water . . .

Balanza

La noche quieta siempre.
El día va y viene.

La noche muerta y alta.
El día con un ala.

La noche sobre espejos
y el día bajo el viento.

Balanza

The night, quiet, always.
The day goes & comes.

The night, tall & dead.
The day with a wing.

The night over a glass
& the day below the wind.

Saeta

Cristo moreno
pasa
de lirio de Judea
a clavel de España.

¡Miradlo por dónde viene!

De España
Cielo limpio y oscuro,
tierra tostada,
y cauces donde corre
muy lenta el agua.
Critso moreno,
con las guedejas quemadas,
los pómulos salientes
y las pupilas blancas.

¡Miradlo por dónde va!

Saeta

The dark Christ
walks from
the iris of Judea to
Spain's pink carnation.

Look there! He's coming!

Spain's
a clean dark sky,
parched land
& drains
where water
runs
very
slowly.

The dark Christ
with scorched locks,
with protruding cheekbones,
the pupils of the eyes, white.

Look! There he goes!

Mar

Abril de 1919

El mar es
el Lucifer del azul.
El cielo caído
por querer ser la luz.

¡Pobre mar condenado
a eterno movimiento,
habiendo antes estado
quieto en el firmamento!

Pero de tu amargura
te redimió el amor.
Pariste a Venus pura,
y quedóse tu hondura
virgen y sin dolor.

Tus tristezas son bellas,
mar de espasmos gloriosos.
Mas hoy en vez de estrellas
tienes pulpos verdosos.

Aguanta tu sufrir,
formidable Satán.
Cristo anduvo por ti,
mas también lo hizo Pan.

La estrella Venus es
la armonía del mundo.
¡Calle el Eclesiastés!
Venus es lo profundo
del alma . . .

. . . Y el hombre miserable
es un ángel caído.
La tierra es el probable
Paraíso perdido.

Sea

1919

The sea is
the Lucifer of blue.
The sky fallen
for wanting to be the light.

Poor sea!   condemned
to eternal movement
having been before
a stillness in the firmament.

But from your bitterness
love redeemed you.
You brought forth Venus
        without blemish
your depth diminished
without travail . virgin .

Your glooms are beautiful, sea,
your glorious spasms.
Besides, today, in place of stars
you have cuttlefish, viridescent.

Formidable Satan
suffers when you suffer.
Christ walked upon you, but
then, so did Pan.

The star Venus is
the world's harmony.
Calle el Eclesiastés!
Venus is the soul-depth of
        the soul . . .
. . . And man, miserable, a
        fallen angel.
And earth is the probable
paradise that was lost.

Nocturnos de la Ventana

A la memoria de José Ciria y Escalante, poeta

1

Alta va la luna.
Bajo corre el viento.

(Mis largas miradas
exploran el cielo.)

Luna sobre el agua.
Luna bajo el viento.

(Mis cortas miradas
exploran el suelo.)

Las voces de dos niñas
venían. Sin esfuerzo,
de la luna del agua
me fuí a la del cielo.

2

Un brazo de la noche
entra por mi ventana.

Un gran brazo moreno
con pulseras de agua.

Sobre un cristal azul
jugaba al río mi alma.

Los instantes heridos
por el reloj . . . pasaban.

Nocturnes: The Window

In memoriam José Ciria y Escalante, poet

1

The moon goes high.
The wind blows down.

> (My long glances
> search the sky.)

Moon over water.
Moon under the wind.

> (My short glances
> search the ground.)

Voices of 2 small girls
were coming. Powerless,
I went from the water's
moon to the sky's moon.

2

An arm of night enters
comes in thru my window.

A great brown arm
with bracelets of water.

Over a blue pool, my
soul played at the river.

And the seconds wounded
by the clock . . .were passing.

3

Asomo la cabeza
por mi ventana, y veo
cómo quiere cortarla
la cuchilla del viento.

En esta guillotina
invisible, yo he puesto
la cabeza sin ojos
de todos mis deseos.

Y un olor de limón
llenó el instante inmenso,
mientras se convertía
en flor de gasa el viento.

4

Al estanque se le ha muerto
hoy una niña de agua.
Está fuera del estanque,
sobre el suelo amortajada.

De la cabeza a sus muslos
un pez la cruza, llamándola.
El viento le dice "niña"
mas no pueden despertarla.

El estanque tiene suelta
su cabellera de algas
y al aire sus grises tetas
estremecidas de ranas.

Dios te salve. Rezaremos
a Nuestra Señora de Agua
por la niña del estanque
muerta bajo las manzanas.

Yo luego pondré a su lado
dos pequeñas calabazas
para que se tenga a flote,
¡ay! sobre la mar salada.

3

I shove my head out
my window and see
how the knife of wind
wants to cut it off.

Into this invisible
guillotine, I've put
the eyeless head of
all my desires.

The smell of lemon
filled an immense second,
while the wind transformed
itself to a gauze blossom.

4

Today, in the reservoir,
a small girl died in the water.
She is out of the lake now,
sheeted and on the ground.

From her head to her thighs
a fish passes over, calling her.
The wind says it : "niña"
but cannot wake her.

The pool has loosened its hair
shocks of weed floating.
In the air, grey are its nipples
terrified, shaken by frogs.

God keep you. We shall
pray to Our Lady of Waters
for the small girl from the pool
dead under the appletrees.

I will put later
two small gourds beside her,
that she may keep herself afloat
hai! on the salt sea.

Anda Jaleo

Yo me subí a un pino verde
por ver si la divisaba
y sólo divisé el polvo
del coche que la llevaba.

Anda jaleo, jaleo;
ya se acabó el alboroto
y ahora empieza el tiroteo.

En la calle de los Muros
mataron a una paloma.
Yo cortaré con mis manos,
las flores de su corona.

Anda jaleo, jaleo;
ya se acabó el alboroto
y ahora empieza el tiroteo.

No salgas, paloma, al campo,
mira que soy cazador
y si te tiro y te mato
para mí será el dolor,
para mí será el quebranto.

Anda jaleo, jaleo;
ya se acabó el alboroto
y ahora empieza el tiroteo.

Hit It!

(Anda Jaleo)

I climbed up
a green pine
to see what I could see
I saw the dust only &
the car that was raising it.

> Go! I cry to the hounds, I cry;
> already the shouting's finished.
> Now the shooting starts.

In the calle de los Muros
they'll kill a dove.
With my hands I'll cut the
flowers for his crown.

> Go! I cry to the hounds, I cry;
> already the shouting's finished.
> Now the shooting starts.

Dove, don't go to the country, recognize
that I am hunter,
& if I shoot & kill you,
mine the pain,
mine will be the loss.

> Go! I cry to the hounds, I cry;
> already the shouting's finished.
> Now the shooting starts.

Los Reyes de la Baraja

Si tu madre quiere un rey,
la baraja tiene cuatro:
rey de oros, rey de copas,
rey de espadas, rey de bastos.

Corre que te pillo,
corre que te agarro,
mira que te lleno
la cara de barro.

Del olivo
me retiro,
del esparto
yo me aparto,
del sarmiento
me arrepiento
de haberte querido tanto.

Kings in the Deck

If your mother wants a king
the deck of cards has 4 :
King of Coins, King of Cups,
King of Swords, King of Clubs.

Run, or I'll grab you,
run or I'll catch you,
look out or I'll stuff
mud in your mouth.

From the olive tree
I walk free.
From *esparto* grass
I shake ass,
& by the vine shoot
I regret
having wanted you so much.

Nana de Sevilla

Este galapaguito
no tiene mare;
lo parió una gitana,
lo echó a la calle.
No tiene mare, sí;
no tiene mare, no;
no tiene mare,
lo echó a la calle.

Este niño chiquito
no tiene cuna;
su padre es carpintero
y le hará una.

Sevilla Slumber Song

This little scallawag
does not have a mother;
gypsy gave birth to him,
threw him in the street.
Has no mother, *si,*
has no mother, *no,*
ain't got no mother, she
threw him in the street.

This tiny fellow
does not have a cradle;
his father is a carpenter
& will make him one.

Huerto de Marzo

Mi manzano
tiene ya sombra y pájaros.

¡Qué brinco da mi sueño
de la luna al viento!

Mi manzano
da a lo verde sus brazos.

¡Desde marzo, cómo veo
le frente blanca de enero!

Mi manzano . . .
(viento bajo).

Mi manzano . . .
(cielo alto).

Orchard in March

My apple tree
has shadow and birds already.

What a leap   my sleep
takes from the moon to the wind!

My apple tree
gives its arms to greenness.

How, after March, January'
s white forehead I see!

My apple tree . . .
(low wind).

My apple tree . . .
(high sky).

La Monja Gitana

A José Moreno Villa

Silencio de cal y mirto.
Malvas en las hierbas finas.
La monja borda alhelíes
sobre una tela pajiza.
Vuelan en la araña gris,
siete pájaros del prisma.
La iglesia gruñe a lo lejos
como un oso panza arriba.
¡Qué bien borda! ¡Con qué gracia!
Sobre la tela pajiza,
ella quisiera bordar
flores de su fantasía.
¡Qué girasol! ¡Qué magnolia
de lentejuelas y cintas!
¡Qué azafranes y qué lunas,
en el mantel de la misa!
Cinco toronjas se endulzan
en la cercana cocina.
Las cinco llagas de Cristo
cortadas en Almería.
Por los ojos de la monja
galopan dos caballistas.
Un rumor último y sordo
le despega la camisa,
y al mirar nubes y montes
en las yertas lejanías,
se quiebra su corazón
de azúcar y yerbaluisa.
¡Oh!, qué llanura empinada
con veinte soles arriba.
¡Qué ríos puestos de pie
vislumbran su fantasía!
Pero sigue con sus flores,
mientras que de pie, en la brisa,
la luz juega el ajedrez
alto de la celosía.

The Gypsy Nun

For José Moreno Villa

Silence of lime & myrtle .
Mallows among delicate herbs .
The nun embroiders gilliflowers
on a straw-colored fabric .
7 birds in a prism
circle in the spider-grey .
The church grunts at the prospect
like a bear with a high stomach .
How well she embroiders! With what grace!
On the straw-colored fabric she
wanted to embroider flowers out
of her fantasy . What
sunflower! What magnolia!
magnolia with spangles & ribbons!
What crocuses & moonflowers!
in the altar-cloth for the mass.
5 grapefruit are ripening
in the kitchen close by .
5 wounds of the Christ
cut open in Almeria.
Through the nun's eyes, a
pair of bandits gallop .
A rustling, final & thin,
escapes the starched fichu,
& to see clouds & mountains
in the motionless distances,
the heart twists in itself
sugar & yerbaluisa . What
an exalted flatland, high
with 20 gold suns above it!
What rivers of foot-tracks
her mind caught glimmering of!
But she continues with her flowers .
Footloose in the breeze,
the lumina plays at chess
high on the window blind .

Canción de las Siete Doncellas

(Teoría del arco iris)

Cantan las siete
doncellas.

(Sobre el cielo un arco
de ejemplos de ocaso.)

Alma con siete voces
las siete doncellas.

En el aire blanco,
siete largos pájaros.)

Mueren las siete
doncellas.

(¿Por qué no han sido nueve?
¿Por qué no han sido veinte?)

El río las trae,
nadie puede verlas.

Song of the 7 Maidens

(A Theory to Explain Rainbows)

They sing
7 donzellas .

> (Across the sky an arc
>   pattern for sunsets)

A soul with 7 voices, the
7 donzellas .

> (In the white air
>   7 great birds)

The 7 donzellas   die

> (Why could they not be 9?
>   Why could they not be 20? !)

The river carries them

> No one
> can see them.

Eco

Ya se ha abierto
la flor de la aurora.

(¿Recuerdas
el fondo de la tarde?

El nardo de la luna
derrama su olor frío.

(¿Recuerdas
la mirada de agosto?)

Echo

Dawn's flower has already
      opened itself
           up .
               (Remember?
               the depths of the afternoon?)

The spikenard of moon diffuses
      its cold smell .
               (Remember?
               the long glance of August?)

Madrigalillo

Cuatro granados
tiene tu huerto.

(Toma mi corazón
nuevo.)

Cuatro cipreses
tendrá tu huerto.

(Toma mi corazón
viejo.)

Sol y luna.
Luego . . .
¡ni corazón
ni huerto!

Small Madrigal

Your orchard has
4 pomegranate trees .

      (Take my new heart)

4 cypresses is what
your orchard will have .

      (Take my old heart)

Sun and moon .
    Then . . .
neither heart nor orchard!

[Zarzamora con el Tronco Gris]

Zarzamora con el tronco gris,
dame un racimo para mí.

Sangre y espinas. Acércate.
Si tú me quieres, yo te querré.

Deja tu fruto de verde y sombra
sobre mi lengua, zarzamora.

Qué largo abrazo te daría
en la penumbra de mis espinas.

Zarzamora, ¿donde vas?
A buscar amores que tú no me das.

Blackberry Bush

Blackberry, with the grey stem, give me
a handful of berries to eat.

Blood & thorns.   Closer!
If you love me, I'll love you.

Leave on my tongue your
fruit of green & shadow,   blackberry .

                        Just think
of the long hug I'll give you within the partial shadow of my thorns .

Blackberry, where're you going?
To look for the loves you don't give
                                me.

[Galán]

Galán,
galancillo.
En tu casa queman tomillo.

Ni que vayas, ni que vengas,
con llave cierro la puerta.

Con llave de plata fina.
Atada con una cinta.

En la cinta hay un letrero:
"Mi corazón está lejos."

No des vueltas en mi calle.
¡Déjasela toda al aire!

Galán,
galancillo.
En tu casa queman tomillo.

Ladies' Man

Lover,
little lover.
At your house they burn thyme & clover.

Tho you neither come in nor go out
I lock the door with a key.
With a key of fine silver
bound, laced with a ribbon.

On the ribbon a text:
"My heart is far from me."

You wouldn't take a turn around my block,
into my street. Go ahead!
Leave it all up in the air!

Lover,
little lover.
They burn thyme & clover at your house.

Canción de Jinete

(1860)

En la luna negra
de los bandoleros,
cantan las espuelas.

Caballito negro.
¿Dónde llevas tu jinete muerto?

. . . Las duras espuelas
del bandido inmóvil
que perdió las riendas.

Caballito frío.
¡Qué perfume de flor de cuchillo!

En la luna negra
sangraba el costado
de Sierra Morena.

Caballito negro.
¿Dónde llevas tu jinete muerto?

La noche espolea
sus negros ijares
clavándose estrellas.

Caballito frío.
¡Qué perfume de flor de cuchillo!

En la luna negra,
¡un grito! y el cuerno
largo de la hoguera.

Caballito negro.
¿Dónde llevas tu jinete muerto?

Canción de Jinete

(1860)

                    In the black
                    moon of the stirrups
                    the spurs sing.

                              Little black horse.
                    Where do you carry your dead rider?

            The hard spurs
            of the unmoving bandit who
            lost the reins.

                              Cold little horse. What a
                    scent of the flower of a knife!

In the black moon
bloody were the spurs
of the Sierra Morena.

                              Little black horse.
                    Where do you carry your dead rider?

The night spurs
its black flanks
nailed with stars.

                              Cold little horse.
                    What a perfume of the flower of a knife!

In the black moon
a yell! and the spur,
the long horn of the bonfire.

                              Little black horse.
                    Where do you carry your dead rider?

Canción de Jinete

Córdoba.
Lejana y sola.

Jaca negra, luna grande,
y aceitunas en mi alforja.
Aunque sepa los caminos
yo nunca llegaré a Córdoba.

Por el llano, por el viento,
jaca negra, luna roja.
La muerte me está mirando
desde las torres de Córdoba.

¡Ay qué camino tan largo!
¡Ay mi jaca valerosa!
¡Ay que la muerte me espera,
antes de llegar a Córdoba!

Córdoba.
Lejana y sola.

Canción de Jinete

Córdoba. Remote
and alone.

Black pony, big moon,
olives in my saddlebag.
Altho I know all the roads,
I will never arrive at Córdoba.

Over the plain, over the wind,
black pony, moon red.
Death is looking at me
down from the towers of Córdoba.

Ai! this road is long!
Ai! my valorous pony!
Ai! that Death awaits me
before I come to Córdoba!

Córdoba. Remote
and alone.

Es Verdad

¡Ay qué trabajo me cuesta
quererte como te quiero!

Por tu amor me duele el aire,
el corazón
y el sombrero.

¿Quién me compraría a mi,
este cintillo que tengo
y esta tristeza de hilo
blanco, para hacer pañuelos?

¡Ay qué trabajo me cuesta
quererte como te quiero!

Es Verdad

Ai, what work it costs me,
wanting you like I want you!

All on account of your love
the air
hurts me —
my heart,
even my hat.

Who will buy it for me,
this hatband I'm holding,
and this sorrow of linen,
white to make handkerchiefs?

Ai! what work it costs me,
wanting you like I want you.

Omega

(poema para muertos)

Las hierbas.
Yo me cortaré la mano derecha.
Espera.
Las hierbas.
Tengo un guante de mercurio y otro de seda.
Espera.
¡Las hierbas!
No solloces. Silencio, que no nos sientan.
Espera.
¡Las hierbas!
Se cayeron las estatuas.
al abrirse la gran puerta.
¡¡Las hierbaaas!!

Omega

(poem for the dead)

Herbs.
I'll cut off my right hand.
Hold it.
The herbs.
I have one glove of mercury & the other of silk.
Hold it.
The herbs!
Don't blubber. Keep quiet, they won't sense us.
Hold it.
Herbs!
The statues fell
at the swinging wide of the great door.
The herrrbs!!

La Soleá

Vestida con mantos negros
piensa que el mundo es chiquito
y el corazón es inmenso.

Vestida con mantos negros.

Piensa que el suspiro tierno
y el grito, desaparecen
en la corriente del viento.

Vestida con mantos negros.

Se dejó el balcón abierto
y al alba por el balcón
desembocó todo el cielo.

¡Ay yayayayay,
que vestida con mantos negros!

The Recluse

Rigged out in black veils
she thinks the world is tiny
& that the heart is immense

   BLACK VEILS

She thinks the delicate sigh
& the scream, will disappear
in the wind-flow

   THOSE BLACK VEILS

Balcón was left open &
at dawn, the whole sky
rushed in at the balcony

MIGOD, WHAT A WAY TO DRESS!
   BLACK VEILS!

Sorpresa

Muerto se quedó en la calle
con un puñal en el pecho.
No lo conocía nadie.
¡Cómo temblaba el farol!
Madre.
¡Cómo temblaba el farolito
de la calle!
Era madrugada. Nadie
pudo asomarse a sus ojos
abiertos al duro aire.
Que muerto se quedó en la calle
que con un puñal en el pecho
y que no lo conocía nadie.

Surprise

The dead man lay in the street
        with a knife in his chest.
No one knew who he was. How
the streetlamp trembled!
           Madre.
How the little streetlamp trembled!
Between the night & the morning. No one
could lean over his eyes open on raw air.
          How come
this dead man lies in the street, what?
with a knife in his chest, & that no
one should know who he was?

Canción de le Muerte Pequeña

Prado mortal de lunas
y sangre bajo tierra.
Prado de sangre vieja.

Luz de ayer y mañana.
Cielo mortal de hierba.
Luz y noche de arena.

Me encontré con la muerte.
Prado mortal de tierra.
Una muerte pequeña.

El perro en el tejado.
Sola mi mano izquierda
atravesaba montes sin fin
de flores secas.

Catedral de ceniza.
Luz y noche de arena.
Una muerte pequeña.

Una muerte y yo un hombre.
Un hombre solo, y ella
una muerte pequeña.

Prado mortal de luna.
La nieve gime y tiembla
por detrás de la puerta.

Un hombre, ¿y qué? Lo dicho.
Un hombre solo y ella.
Prado, amor, luz y arena.

Song of the Small Dead Girl

Meadow of moons, mortal
& blood below the earth.
Meadow of old blood.

Yesterday's light & tomorrow's.
Sky of herbs, mortal.
Light & night of sand.

I found myself with the girl.
Mortal meadow of earth.
A small dead girl.

The dog in the shed.
My lonely left hand passed
over endless mountains
of dried flowers.

Cathedral of ashes.
Light & night of sand.
A small dead girl.

A dead girl & I, a man.
A man alone & her
a small dead girl.

Mortal meadow of moon.
Snow   moans & trembles
outside the door.

A man & what?   I said it.
A man alone & her.
Meadow & love,
light & sand.

Refrán

Marzo
pasa volando.

Y Enero sigue tan alto.

Enero,
sigue en la noche del cielo.

Y abajo Marzo es un momento.

Enero.
Para mis ojos viejos.

Marzo.
Para mis frescas manos.

Saying

March
passes flying.

And January follows so high.

    January,
follows in the night of the sky.

And below, March is a second.

    January.
For my old eyes.

    March.
For my fresh hands.

Adelina de Paseo

La mar no tiene naranjas,
ni Sevilla tiene amor.
Morena, qué luz de fuego
Préstame tu quitasol.

Me pondrá la cara verde
— zumo de lima y limón —,
tus palabras — pececillos —
nadarán alrededor.

La mar no tiene naranjas.
Ay, amor.
¡Ni Sevilla tiene amor!

Saturday Paseo: Adelina

Oranges
do not grow in the sea
anymore than there's love in Sevilla.
      Dark one, the sun's that hot, I'm—
        loan me your parasol.

I'll wear my jealous expression,
all lemon & lime juice—
      your words,
    sinful little words—
will swim around it a bit.

Oranges
do not grow in the sea,
ay, love!
      And there's no love in Sevilla!

Cazador

¡Alto pinar!
Cuatro palomas por el aire van.

Cuatro palomas
vuelan y tornan.
Llevan heridas
sus cuatro sombras.

¡Bajo pinar!
Cuatro palomas en la tierra están.

Hunter

High the pine grove!
Thru the air
4 pigeons.

4 pigeons turn
return. Their 4 shadows
carry wounds.

Low the pine grove!
On the ground
4 pigeons.

Fábula

Unicornios y cíclopes.

Cuernos de oro
y ojos verdes.

Sobre el acantilado,
en tropel gigantesco,
ilustran el azogue
sin cristal, del mar.

Unicornios y cíclopes.

Una pupila
y una potencia.
¿Quién duda la eficacia
terrible de esos cuernos?
¡Oculta tus blancos,
Naturaleza!

Fable

Unicorns & cyclopes.

Gold horns
& green eyes.

On the sheer bluff
they illustrate
in a monstrous herd
quicksilver of the sea
no crystal.

Unicorns & cyclopes.

An eyeball
& a power.
Who is there doubts the terrible
efficacy of those horns?

World,
hide your targets!

Cortaron Tres Árboles

a Ernesto Halffter

Eran tres.
(Vino el día con sus hachas.)
Eran dos.
(Alas rastreras de plata.)
Era uno.
Era ninguno.
(Se quedó desnuda el agua.)

They Cut Down Three Trees

(for Ernesto Halffter)

There were three.
(The day came with its hatchets.)
There were two.
(Wings traced with silver.)
There was one.
There were none.
(Just the naked water.)

[Agosto]

Agosto.
Contraponientes
de melocotón y azúcar,
y el sol dentro de la tarde,
como el hueso en una fruta.

La panocha guarda intacta
su risa amarilla y dura.

Agosto.
Los niños comen
pan moreno y rica luna.

[August]

August.
Counterpoints.
sugar & peach, and
the sun in the afternoon
like the pit in a fruit.

The corn keeps intact
its smile, yellow, hard.

August.
The kids eat
dark bread, rich moon.

Canción China en Europa

a mi ahijada Isabel Clara

La señorita
del abanico,
va por el puente
del fresco río.

Los caballeros
con sus levitas,
miran el puente
sin barandillas.

La señorita
del abanico,
y los volantes,
busca marido.

Los caballeros
están casados,
con altas rubias
de idioma blanco.

Los grillos cantan
por el Oeste.

(La señorita,
va por lo verde.)

Los grillos cantan
bajo las flores.

(Los caballeros,
van por el Norte.)

Chinese Song in Europe

for my goddaughter Isabel Clara

>   The young lady
> with the fan
> goes over the bridge
> at the cool river.

>   The gentlemen
> wearing smocks
> look at the bridge
> without handrails.

>   The young lady
> with the fans & veils
> is looking for
> a husband.

>   The gentlemen
> are married
> to tall blondes
> with white speech.

>   The crickets sing
> in the west.

(The young lady
>   goes toward the green.)

The crickets sing
under the flowers.

>   (The gentlemen
go north.)

Cancioncilla Sevillana

a Solita Salinas

Amanecía
en el naranjel.
Abejitas de oro
buscaban la miel.

¿Dónde estará
la miel?

Está en la flor azul,
Isabel.
En la flor,
del romero aquel.

(Sillita de oro
para el moro.
Silla de oropel
para su mujer.)

Amanecía
en el naranjel.

Small Song from Sevilla

for Solita Salinas

Daybreak
in the orange grove.
Little golden bees
were looking for honey.

Where will
the honey be?

In the blue flower,
Isabel.
In the flower of
the rosemary there.

(Little gold chair
for the moor.
Tinsel chair
for his wife.)

   Dawn was breaking
in the orange grove.

Caracola

a Natalita Jiménez

Me han traído una caracola.

Dentro le canta
un mar de mapa.
Mi corazón
se llena de agua
con pececillos
de sombra y plata.

Me han traído una caracola.

Caracola

for Natalia Jiménez

They've brought me a shell.

It sings inside
a sea on a map.
My heart
fills up with water
with little fish
shadow & silver.

They've
brought me a shell.

Gacela del Amor Imprevisto

Nadie comprendía el perfume
de la oscura magnolia de tu vientre.
Nadie sabía que martirizabas
un colibrí de amor entre los dientes.

Mil caballitos persas se dormían
en la plaza con luna de tu frente,
mientras que yo enlazaba cuatro noches
tu cintura, enemiga de la nieve.

Entre yeso y jazmines, tu mirada
era un pálido ramo de simientes.
Yo busqué, para darte, por mi pecho
las letras de marfil que dicen *siempre*,

siempre, siempre: jardín de mi agonía,
tu cuerpo fugitivo para siempre,
la sangre de tus venas en mi boca,
tu boca ya sin luz para mi muerte.

Gacela of the Unexpected Love

No one understood the fragrance
of your belly's dark magnolia.
No one knew you were martyring
a loving hummingbird between your teeth.

A 1000 persian horses were sleeping
in the plaza, with the moon of your forehead,
while for four nights I held
enemy of the snow, your waist.

Your glance between gypsum and jasmin,
between the white wall and the flowers,
was a pallid branch of seeds.
I searched about my chest to give you
the ivory letters reading *siempre,*

siempre, siempre: garden of my agony,
your fugitive body for — always,
the blood of your veins in my mouth,
darkness of your mouth for my death.

Gacela de la Terrible Presencia

Yo quiero que el agua se quede sin cauce.
Yo quiero que el viento se quede sin valles.

Quiero que la noche se quede sin ojos
y mi corazón sin la flor del oro;

que los bueyes hablen con las grandes hojas
y que la lombriz se muera de sombra;

que brillen los dientes de la calavera
y los amarillos inunden la seda.

Puedo ver el duelo de la noche herida
luchando enroscada con el mediodía.

Resisto un ocaso de verde veneno
y los arcos rotos donde sufre el tiempo.

Pero no ilumines tu limpio desnudo
como un negro cactus abierto en los juncos.

Déjame en un ansia de oscuros planetas,
pero no me enseñes tu cintura fresca.

Gacela of the Awful Presence

I want the water to stay without pipes.
I want the wind to stay without valleys.

I want the night to remain without eyes
and my heart without the golden flower;

the oxen to talk with the big leaves,
and the worm to die from the shadow;

that the teeth glitter from the skull
and all yellows to flood over silk.

I can see the duel of night wounded,
struggling, twisted with midday.

I resist a west of green poison,
the broken arches under which the time suffers.

But do not show the light your clean nakedness,
a black cactus standing open in the garbage pits.

Quit me in the anxiety of dark planets, but do
not teach me the freshness of your waist.